Made in United States
Troutdale, OR
01/17/2024

16981741R00058